MW01131728

Green Card Voices
2822 Lyndale Avenue South
Minneapolis, MN 55408
phone: 612.889.7635
fax: 612.871.6927

Printed in the United States of America

Green Card Voices, 2015

ISBN-10: 0692572813

ISBN-13: 9780692572818

31009470

www.greencardvoices.org

DEDICATION

This teaching guide is dedicated to future generations of immigrants and all newcomers to the United States. May you find freedom and opportunity without discrimination.

ACKNOWLEDGEMENTS

Over the past two years, the stories that Green Card Voices (GCV) has recorded have entered many classrooms throughout Minnesota and the greater United States. We soon realized that our work could be amplified by providing classroom teachers a framework and tools that place the first-person immigrant stories in the center of the learning process. As a result we created this teaching guide to assist teachers who want to learn and teach about a wide range of immigration topics through first-person storytelling. We would like to thank countless educators who voiced their urgent desire to teach about immigration in a new, more relevant and effective way. You shared with us your concerns about the changing demographics in the population of your classroom and that you lacked resources to teach about that change in a positive way. You also shared with us that when creating lessons for teachers they need to be in line with National and State Standards for you to be able to use them. We listened!

This teaching guide would not be possible without the 126 immigrant storytellers who have shared their stories with Green Card Voices over the past few years. Eleven of the stories are included in this teaching guide: Nickolai Kolarov (Bulgaria), Nachito Herrera (Cuba), Ikhlaq Hussain (Pakistan), Shegitu Kebede (Ethiopia), Ruhel Islam (Bangladesh), Barbara G. Pierre-Louis (Haiti), Mary Gorše Manning (Slovenia), Miguel Ramos (Puerto Rico), Ibrahim Hirsi (Somalia), Kushe Saw (Burma), and Irma Marquez Trapero (Mexico). Their courage inspires us all; they are the heart and soul of this work.

There are several individuals who have been instrumental in creating this teaching guide. First, we would like to thank our curriculum developer and lead author, Veronica Quillien. A "third culture kid" and first generation immigrant from Cameroon, she drew from her life experiences and educational background to create an engaging and interactive curriculum. Currently she is pursuing a Ph.D. in Curriculum and Instruction at the University of Minnesota. We could not be more pleased with her creative, original, and cutting edge approach to the teaching guide.

Next, we would like to thank Tea Rozman Clark, Ph.D., the Executive Director of Green Card Voices. She shared immigrant stories with many classrooms in Minnesota. In addition to her many presentations, she interviewed over 120 immigrants and oversaw the entire recording, editing, and publishing of the GCV storytelling process. Ms. Rozman Clark is herself a first generation immigrant from Slovenia. She worked with Veronica Quillien every step of the way to create a teaching guide that is inclusive and respectful to all immigrant storytellers and addresses present-day issues in the classroom. As the editor-in-chief of the publication, she also dealt with content, copyright, and finances.

Kathy Seipp also edited and revised this teaching guide throughout the writing process. As a board member of Green Card Voices she brought an incredible array of expertise and knowledge to make this project a success. As a current classroom teacher she ensured that the lessons are teacher-friendly, sensitive to the diverse immigrant backgrounds in classrooms (from adopted children, to those who are refugees themselves, to those who are undocumented) as well as the needs of teachers. In her own classroom and school she has already seen how the GCV stories can impact the school and its community in a short period of time. Kathy is also the co-author of "Energy of a Nation: Immigrants in America" 3rd Ed. (published 2008).

ACKNOWLEDGEMENTS CONT.

A tremendous thank you goes to Jose Guzman, who edited and illustrated the teaching guide. Jose has worked for Green Card Voices as a writer, video editor, and graphic designer. As a second generation American, with parents from Central America, he has been an integral part of every facet of the organization.

We extend gratitude and thanks to Rachel Mueller who edited and prepared the teaching guide for publication. Her experience of writing, editing, and publishing has made her an invaluable part of our team. In addition to her work on this project, she conducts evaluation research for Green Card Voices.

This teaching guide would not exist if not for the generous support of several organizations. First and foremost, we would like to thank the University of Minnesota's Center for Urban and Regional Affairs (CURA). Their grant through the Kris Nelson Community Based Research Program was instrumental in funding this project and allowed us to hire our curriculum developer, Veronica Quillien. We also extend our gratitude to the Education Minnesota Foundation, which has been a supporter of GCV in Schools and all of our educational resources.

In addition, there are several other companies, foundations, and individuals that have contributed to Green Card Voices and this teaching guide. They include: The Minneapolis Foundation; The Marbrook Foundation; The Bush Foundation, Microgrants; Hemisphere Companies; Minnesota Twins Baseball Club; Fredrikson and Byron, P.A.; Gandhi Mahal; Prudent Accountants; Dorsey and Whitney; Intermedia Arts; India Association of Minnesota; and the International Institute of Minnesota.

Lastly, there are several additional people and organizations that have contributed to the success of Green Card Voices. Our work has thrived due to their tremendous encouragement and support. We would like to thank our past and present Green Card Voices board members, Neha Belvalkar, Evelyn Arevalo-Hernandez, Jean-Baptiste Quillien and all others who have helped our mission along the way.

KHÀWP JAI. GRACIAS. NGIYABONGA. HVALA. XIÈXIE. MAMNUNAM. DÍK. TÄNAN. VINAKA. MERCI. EFHARISTÓ. ARIGATO. KAMSAHAMNIDA. SIPAS. BAYARLALAA. DHANYABAD. TASHAKOR. DZIEKI. OBRIGADO. SPASIBO. DAKUJEM. MAHADSANID. ASANTE. SALAMAT PO. KÒP KUN. TESEKKÜR EDERIM. XIN CAM ON. NGIYABONGA. DHANYAVAD. SHUKRAN. DHONNOBAD. MATUR NUWUN. IMELA. O SE. TAWDI SAGI. GMADLOBT. RAV TODOT. UA TSAUG.

Thank You.

WHY THIS TEACHING GUIDE?

Immigration is an important symbol of the United States. Immigrants have played a vital role at each turn in our nation's history, and continue to do so today. Green Card Voices (GCV), a nonprofit organization based in Minneapolis, MN, has captured stories of recent immigrants to the U.S. in order to instill a sense of pride in our nation's immigrant population and to bridge the gap between the immigrant and non-immigrant communities.

GCV's digital stories provide a rich collection of immigrant voices and experiences. They are dynamic and designed to engage participants. Students will be able to better understand, respond to, and accommodate the cultural dimensions of fellow students who are new to the U.S. Teachers will learn how to be more inclusive and welcoming towards the ever-changing face of America's youth and help build cultural connections among different students. Exploring opinions about immigration in the classroom challenges commonly held myths and prepares students to grapple with different cultural issues in a respectful, thoughtful, and productive way. Moreover, integrating the facts and stories of immigrant experiences into classrooms and the school helps to create a more welcoming environment for new immigrant students and their families, as they see that their knowledge and experiences are valued.

WHO IS THIS TEACHING GUIDE FOR?

The purpose of this teaching guide is to enrich classroom instruction around the topic of immigration by using alternative methods to stimulate students' learning. It is intended for grades 6 through 12.

EACH LESSON WILL INCLUDE:

1. Focus	5. Objectives
2. Core standards	6. Materials
3. Essential Question	7. Instruction
4. Timeframe	8. Reflections/Notes

CORE STANDARDS

We purposefully chose the Common Core standards over the state standards as they are a reference for Social Studies teachers across the nation. Therefore, activities are aligned with core standards from the National Council for Social Studies, which teachers can then align with state standards.

THE CORE STANDARDS ARE:

I. Culture and Cultural Diversity	VI. Power, Authority, and Governance
II. Time, Continuity, and Change	VII. Production, Distribution, and Consumption
III. People, Places, and Environments	VIII. Science, Technology, and Society
IV. Individual Development and Identity	IX. Global Connections
V. Individuals, Groups, and Institutions	X. Civic Ideals and Practices

A DEVELOPMENTAL FRAMEWORK

The goal of this curriculum is for students to feel a sense of pride that the United States is a nation of immigrants. We decided to use a developmental approach for this curriculum. The topic of immigration is introduced from a non-threatening perspective, and gradually builds on a foundational understanding of immigration. First, students will look at the icons of immigration, such as Ellis Island. Then they will draft their own immigrant story. Afterward, we softly introduce several facets of culture, such as music and food. As students gain awareness, we continuously introduce new topics that will challenge them to think about how they can make new immigrants feel welcome in their school and, in the end, encourage them to think about larger immigration issues.

TABLE OF CONTENTS

FOCUS

- Pathways for people to immigrate to the United States
- Watch Mary Gorše Manning GCV video about her arrival at Ellis Island

OBJECTIVES

- Students will conduct research on immigration paths
- Students will report on their findings
- Students will be able to name immigration paths
- Students will write a proposal to explore a new story

ESSENTIAL QUESTIONS

- How do people immigrate to the U.S.?
- Where are immigrants from?

CORE STANDARDS

I. Culture and Cultural Diversity

II. Time, Continuity, and Change

IV. Individual Development and Identity

GRADE LEVEL

6TH-12TH

TIME FRAME

1-2 CLASS PERIODS

SUGGESTIONS:

- 10 MINUTES TO WATCH GCV VIDEO
- 40 MINUTES FOR RESEARCH AND SUMMARY

MATERIALS

- LEARNERS NOTEBOOK
- PEN, PENCILS
- GCV MARY GORŠE MANNING VIDEO AND PROFILE
- IMMIGRANT STORY WORKSHEET

VIDEO LINKS

MARY GORŠE MANNING
www.greencardvoices.com/speakers/mary-gorse-manning/

INSTRUCTIONS

LESSON 1

BEFORE

FOR TEACHER: IF USING THE SUGGESTED QUESTIONS, RESEARCH THE ANSWERS PRIOR CLASS

1. Ask students about the Statue of Liberty (use the following suggested questions).

- What does the statue represent?
- Who built the statue and why?
- Where is the statue located?
- Has anyone in the class seen it?

DURING

2. Have students watch the GCV video of Mary Gorše Manning. As a class, go through the **VIDEO CONTENT DISCUSSION** questions. You may need to watch the video multiple times.

3. Have students research the following immigration paths. PLEASE SEE RESOURCE LIST.

   Ellis Island – Who mainly immigrated through Ellis Island?

   Angel Island – Who mainly immigrated through Angel Island?

   African American Registry – How did African Americans immigrate to the United States?

AFTER

4. For next class, give the assignment below:

   a. Explore the life story of another person. Students make a proposal for the story of their choosing (their own story, a family friend's story, a neighbor's story, or a story on the Green Card Voices website).

   b. To report on the new story, students can write a half page summary, make a drawing, song, or report in a different format.

VIDEO CONTENT DISCUSSION

LESSON 1

1. Describe Ms. Manning's life in the camp after leaving Slovenia.

2. What were the immigration rules?

3. How did Ms. Manning's family immigrate to the United States?

4. What transportation did her family use to travel to the United States?

5. What was Ms. Manning's life like during the voyage?

6. What were the rules for food when crossing borders?

7. Where did Ms. Manning arrive when she first entered the United States?

8. What were the living conditions in Minneapolis?

9. Describe Ms. Manning's current family.

RESOURCE LIST

National Park Service
www.nps.gov/findapark/index.htm

The Statue of Liberty & Ellis Island
www.libertyellisfoundation.org

Ellis Island, History Channel
www.history.com/topics/ellis-island

History Channel
www.history.com

NPR on 1965 Immigration Act
n.pr/1Mwo8UP

Angel Island
angelisland.org

Immigration, Scholastic
bit.ly/1DMmYfD

African American Registry
www.aaregistry.org

Slavery, PBS
to.pbs.org/Z5Cfum

NOTES:

It might be helpful for students to start a vocabulary list. This list can then be used as a great extra credit opportunity if you chose to do a vocabulary quiz.

Example:

Genealogy
Ancestry
Ellis Island

Profile:
MARY GORŠE MANNING

FROM: Dolenja Vas Pri Ribnici, Slovenia   CURRENT CITY: Minneapolis, MN
OCCUPATION: Retiree

Mary Gorše Manning possesses few pleasant memories of her home country of Slovenia. After a life filled with constant fear, she is grateful for the opportunities her new home has offered.

Born in 1935, the majority of Ms. Gorše Manning's childhood took place amidst the Italian and German occupation of Slovenia during the Second World War. Although the fighting ended in 1945, a new battle "had just begun." Mary's family left Slovenia and headed towards Austria. Her family was relocated to a displaced persons camp—or DP camp—in the city of Spittal where they lived for four years.

During her time in the DP camp, Ms. Gorše Manning enjoyed spending time with other children at the camp's school. They performed plays and did other activities to help detract from the harsh conditions of the camp. As countries gradually began accepting these families for resettlement, Mary's family decided to immigrate to the United States with her aunt as a sponsor. In 1949, Ms. Gorše Manning boarded a boat and set sail for the U.S. Although some aspects of the boat ride were uncomfortable, she was surrounded by more food than any previous time in her life. Eleven days later, she arrived at Ellis Island in New York.

During her time in the United States, Mary graduated high school, worked with National Supermarkets, started a family, and has since retired. She lives in Minneapolis, Minnesota with her husband. They have seven children and eighteen grandchildren.

Dolenja Vas, Slovenia

Name: _____

Date: _____

IMMIGRANT STORY WORKSHEET

I listened to the story of...	
S/he was born in city/country/continent...	
The reason(s) s/he left the country of origin	
Education completed in the country of origin and in the U.S.	
Who s/he left behind; who came with to the U.S.	
Current Occupation	

What was his/her biggest surprise when s/he came to the U.S.?

How did s/he cope with the new environment?

How does s/he contribute to the new homeland?

LESSON 2: I AM HERE AND I MATTER

FOCUS

- Learn about one's heritage
- Conduct an interview
- Re-watch Mary Gorše Manning GCV video

OBJECTIVES

- Students will construct their story
- Students will conduct an interview

ESSENTIAL QUESTIONS

- What are the differences in immigration stories?
- What can we learn from our immigration story/adoption story/ neighbor's story?

CORE STANDARDS

I. Culture and Cultural Diversity

II. Time, Continuity, and Change

IV. Individual Development and Identity

GRADE LEVEL
6th-12th

TIME FRAME
1-2 class periods

MATERIALS

- Learners notebook
- Pen, pencils
- GCV Mary Gorše Manning video and profile
- Immigrant Story Worksheet
- Interview Qustions

INSTRUCTIONS

LESSON 2

BEFORE

1. Have students re-watch Mary Gorše Manning's video.

2. Suggested questions for students. Consider re-wording the questions for adoptees, refugees, etc. (Be sensitive to reliving trauma for refugee students):

- What's your story?
- Who has grandparents?
  - Do you know their story?
  - Did they immigrate to the U.S? When? Why?
- Whose great grandparents are still alive?
  - Did they immigrate to the U.S.? When? Why?

DURING

3. Students will answer the following questions in class (consider adapting questions below for adoptees, refugees, etc.).

- Who are your ancestors?
- What is your family genealogy?
- What's your story?

4. Have students fill out out their immigrant worksheet based on the information they've collected from previous homework and questions above.

AFTER

5. For next class, give assignment below and decide on due date (before Lesson 5):

a. Distribute interview questions to students (consider adapting interview questions for adoptees).

b. The clue to finding answers to the questions above is to talk to their family (parents, grandparents, great-grandparents, uncles, aunties, cousins, family friends, neighbors, etc.).

c. Students should have a conversation with an adult relative on either and/or both sides of their family.

d. When students conduct interviews, use the questions in the handout to guide in your inquisitiveness.

6. For the next lesson, ask students to bring mats, blankets, pillows, bean bags or anything that helps them relax. The next lesson involves listening to relaxing music.

Name: _____

Date: _____

IMMIGRANT STORY WORKSHEET

I listened to the story of...	
S/he was born in city/country/continent...	
The reason(s) s/he left the country of origin	
Education completed in the country of origin and in the U.S.	
Who s/he left behind; who came with to the U.S.	
Current Occupation	

What was his/her biggest surprise when s/he came to the U.S.?

How did s/he cope with the new environment?

How does s/he contribute to the new homeland?

Name: _____

Date: _____

INTERVIEW QUESTIONS

1. Do you know what country our family originally came to the U.S. from?

2. Do you know the name of the ancestors who decided to leave that country?

3. When did they leave? How old were they at that time?

4. Do you know what were the conditions in the country when they left?

5. Did they have time to prepare for the trip?

6. Were they alone when they immigrated?

7. Did they leave anyone behind?

8. Do you know how they got here (boat, plane, etc.)?

9. Did they stay somewhere else before arriving here?

10. Why did they choose the United States?

11. Why didn't they choose another country?

12. What language did they speak?

LESSON **3**: THE FIFTH ELEMENTS

FOCUS

- Exposure to different music
- Exploring different senses
- Watch GCV Videos of Nickolai Kolarov, Nachito Herrera and Ikhlaq Hussain

OBJECTIVES

- Students will observe and explain their reactions to different music
- Students will complete the **5TH ELEMENTS** worksheets

ESSENTIAL QUESTIONS

- How do we deal with differences in our world?
- How does the body respond to different music?

CORE STANDARDS

I. Culture and Cultural Diversity

III. People, Places, and Environments

IX. Global Connections

GRADE LEVEL

6TH-12TH

TIME FRAME

1-3 CLASS PERIODS

MATERIALS

PROFILES OF NICKOLAI KOLAROV, NACHITO HERRERA, IKHLAQ HUSSAIN

- EYE-COVER/SLEEP MASK/ BANDANAS

- RELAXATION MUSIC FROM YOUTUBE

- SELECT YOUTUBE MUSIC FROM

  o NICKOLAI KOLAROV

  o NACHITO HERRERA

  o IKHLAQ HUSSAIN

  THE 5TH ELEMENTS— INSTRUMENTAL WORKSHEET

  THE 5TH ELEMENTS — VIDEO
- WORKSHEET

  IMMIGRANT STORY
- WORKSHEET

VIDEO LINKS

NACHITO HERRERA
www.greencardvoices.com/speakers/nachito-herrera/

NICKOLAI KOLAROV
www.greencardvoices.com/speakers/nickolai-kolarov/

IKHLAQ HUSSAIN
www.greencardvoices.com/speakers/ikhlaq-hussain

INSTRUCTIONS

For this lesson:

Change your room layout to create space for mats, blankets, pillows, bean bags – assign this task to 2-4 students.

Each student must find a place to relax.

FORM GROUPS

Form 3 groups based on which video students watched as homework for **LESSON 2**. If homework wasn't assigned, form 3 groups any way you wish.

In 3-5 minutes, students share their **IMMIGRANT STORY** worksheets they had for homework and create one sheet that captures all participants' ideas. Groups will give 2 minute presentations on their findings.

BEFORE

1. Play the relaxation music you found online for the students.

- Give them 5 minutes to read **THE 5TH ELEMENTS INSTRUMENTAL** worksheet.

- Ask students to get comfortable, put on their eye-cover/bandana/cloth.

- Instruct learners to breathe deeply (inhale for 5 seconds – exhale for 5 seconds). Repeat until you can observe that all students are relaxed.

Page 12

INSTRUCTIONS

DURING

2. Switch from the relaxation music to one of the GCV musicians (Nickolai Kolarov, Nachito Herrera or Ikhlaq Hussain). Check for sound with students; be sure all students are able to hear.

3. Play the song a second time and tell students to fill out **THE 5TH ELEMENTS *INSTRUMENTAL*** worksheet. Once all students are done filling out the worksheet, ask them to fold the worksheet and put away everything.

4. Watch the GCV video of the musician you listened to in step 3. Have students to fill out **THE 5TH ELEMENTS *VIDEO*** worksheet during the video.

4. Repeat steps 3-4 until you have gone through all three musicians.

5. Go through the **VIDEO CONTENT DISCUSSION** questions as a class.

AFTER

6. At the end of the activity, instruct students to:

● Finish all of their worksheets

● Come prepared the following class period to share their thoughts with the class

Nachito Herrera | Cuba
Pianist | Minneapolis, MN

GREEN CARD
VOICES

HOMEWORK

Watch the following stories:

● Ruhel Islam

● Shegitu Kedebe

● Barbara Pierre-Louis

● Teacher's choice

Fill out an Immigration Story Worksheet for each video.

MR. KOLAROV - Cello

Where is Mr. Kolarov from?
What instrument does Mr. Kolarov play?
What happened to Mr. Kolarov after the fall of the Berlin wall?
When did Mr. Kolarov first travel to the United States?
How long did it take until Mr. Kolarov reunited with his wife?
What type of visa does Mr. Kolarov have? Is he a US citizen?
How many children does Mr. Kolarov have?
How did Mr. Kolarov contribute to the University of Minnesota?

MR. HERRERA - Piano

Where is Mr. Herrera from?
Where did Mr. Herrera have his first musical performance?
What happen with Mr. Herrera's cultural exchange visa?
What's an O1 visa?
Who is Carlos Santana?
What award did Mr. Herrera receive?
What are Mr. Herrera contributions to the United States?

MR. HUSSAIN - Sitar

Where is Mr. Hussain from?
Was Mr. Hussain able to be an artist in Pakistan?
How was Mr. Hussain able to learn to play sitar?
Where did Mr. Hussain first perform when he first came to the United States?
What adjective does Mr. Hussain use to describe his first experience?
What are some of the cultural difference Mr. Hussain noticed?
Where did Mr. Hussain hold concerts?
How does Mr. Hussain contribute to the United States?

Profile:
NICKOLAI KOLAROV

FROM: Sofia, Bulgaria   CURRENT CITY: St. Paul, MN
OCCUPATION: Musician and Instructor

Throughout his life, Nickolai Kolarov has devoted much of his time sharing his love for Balkan chamber and folk music. After immigrating to the United States, he views himself as an ambassador to Balkan culture.

Born in Sofia, Bulgaria, Mr. Kolarov developed a love for music at an early age. As a cellist with the Bulgarian Youth Orchestra, he performed in venues around the world including the UN and the National Palace of Culture, Bulgaria's largest performance hall.

After the fall of the Berlin Wall, Nickolai looked for better educational and economic opportunities abroad. He was offered a scholarship to the University of Missouri, Kansas City to complete a master's degree and temporarily left his wife and infant daughter to pursue his dream. Four years later, he was reunited with his family and, they moved to Minnesota where Nickolai completed a doctorate in cello performance.

Mr. Kolarov is the artistic director for Balkanicus—a contemporary Balkan chamber music ensemble. He has received countless awards, including four grants from the Minnesota Metropolitan Regional Arts Council. Additionally, he taught music at the University of St. Thomas and has given lectures at several institutions, including the University of Iowa and the Julliard School. He continues to conduct, teach, and perform across the country.

For additional information, visit: www.musicofthebalkans.weebly.com

Profile:
NACHITO HERRERA

FROM: Santa Clara, Cuba CURRENT CITY: White Bear Lake, MN
OCCUPATION: Musician

Nachito Herrara had rarely considered emigrating from Cuba; a world-renowned pianist, he regularly toured the United States for months at a time – why would he want to change his citizenship? But when the U.S.-Cuba cultural exchange was terminated, he lost freedoms he had grown accustomed to. Nachito's wife called from Havana and told him to stay in Minneapolis.

Mr. Herrera, a child prodigy, frequently put aside new toys to practice piano when he was young. His formal musical tutelage began at the age of seven under the renowned Jorge Gómez Labraña. This classical training fused with his passion for Latin jazz over time, creating his distinctive sound.

After deciding to reside in the United States, Nachito was separated from his family for several years – the events of 9/11 delayed the reunion further. And though his wife and two children were able to join him eventually, his immediate family's separation from their extended family in Cuba remains a sorrowful component of their life in the United States.

Despite these challenges, Mr. Herrera is incredibly grateful for opportunities the United States provides him. He doesn't see himself solely as a musician and teacher; he sees himself as a role model for future generations of musicians. In this vein, he and his wife started the Nachito Herrera Foundation – an organization that provides scholarships to underprivileged immigrant children desiring to learn music.

For additional information, visit: www.nachitoherrera.com.

Santa Clara, Cuba

Profile:
IKHLAQ HUSSAIN

FROM: Karachi, Pakistan   CURRENT CITY: New York, NY
OCCUPATION: Musician and Instructor

Music has been in Ikhlaq Hussain's family for generations. But after the dictator Muhammad Zia-ul-Haq came to power in Pakistan, the country's policies towards music and art became dramatically restrictive.

Mr. Hussain grew up in Karachi, Pakistan. He learned to play sitar from maestros like his father, Ustad Imdad Hussain, and the legendary Pandit Ravi Shankar. At the age of fourteen, Ikhlaq performed in his first concert. His first visit to the U.S. came during a concert series where he performed in Portland, Chicago, Boston, and New York. Astounded by the applause and appreciation he received from his American audiences, Ikhlaq knew he would return someday. He received a visa in 2001, but his family urged him to remain in Pakistan after the attacks on the World Trade Center. After much deliberation, Ikhlaq decided to give life in the U.S. a chance.

Upon his arrival, Mr. Hussain had a difficult time finding a job where he could perform his beloved music. While he had an established career in Pakistan, he soon realized he would have to start over in his new home. Reluctantly, he took a job as a musician in a restaurant. In the following years, Ikhlaq performed at venues such as Central Park and Harvard University.

Currently, Ikhlaq continues to perform across the globe and passes his musical heritage on to future generations by teaching a variety of students. He lives in New York with his wife.

For additional information, visit: www.ragasitar.com

Karachi, Pakistan

Worksheet:
THE 5TH ELEMENTS — INSTRUMENTAL

My experience watching the video of _____.

BRIEF EXPLANATION. Write a few sentences describing the music that you hear.

ATTENDING TO JUDGMENT

1. What is the positive or negative judgment I am having about the song I am listening to?

2. What assumptions am I making about the song I am listening to?

3. What was I expecting?

ATTENDING TO EMOTION

1. What are the positive or negative emotions I am having about this song?

2. How is the melody making me feel?

3. How is the beat making me feel?

4. What is this song telling me about my emotions?

LESSON 3

ATTENDING TO PHYSICAL SENSATION

What is the physical sensation I'm experiencing while listening to this song?

What is the sensation communicating to me?

CULTIVATING STILLNESS

Taking a breath, what did I feel from the silence within?

What can learn about myself from this song?

WHAT ARE MY MIND AND MY HEART CONFUSED ABOUT?

Do I have any questions about this song?

What can I do to learn more about this song?

WHAT DID I LEARN? [WRITE A BRIEF NARRATIVE ABOUT THE EXPERIENCE OF LISTENING TO THE SONG.]

Adapted from Critical Moment Dialogue. MAIR 223 Personal Leadership (template).
Portland, Oregon: The Intercultural Communication Institute.

Worksheet:
THE 5TH ELEMENTS — VIDEO

My experience engaging the video of _____.

BRIEF EXPLANATION. Write a few sentences describing the music that you hear.

ATTENDING TO JUDGMENT

1. What is the positive or negative judgment I am having about the song I am listening to?

2. What assumptions am I making about the song I am listening to?

3. What was I expecting?

ATTENDING TO EMOTION

1. What are the positive or negative emotions I am having about this song?

2. How is the melody making me feel?

3. How is the beat making me feel?

4. What is this song telling me about my emotions?

ATTENDING TO PHYSICAL SENSATION

What is the physical sensation I'm experiencing while listening to this song?

What is the sensation communicating to me?

CULTIVATING STILLNESS

Taking a breath, what did I feel from the silence within?

What can learn about myself from this song?

WHAT ARE MY MIND AND MY HEART CONFUSED ABOUT?

Do I have any questions about this song?

What can I do to learn more about this song?

WHAT DID I LEARN? [WRITE A BRIEF NARRATIVE ABOUT THE EXPERIENCE OF LISTENING TO THE SONG.]

Adapted from Critical Moment Dialogue. MAIR 223 Personal Leadership (template).
Portland, Oregon: The Intercultural Communication Institute.

FOCUS

- Expand curiosity through spices
- Understand the self as a cultural being
- Watch GCV videos or Ruhel Islam, Shegitu Kebede, Barbara Pierre-Louis, and a teacher's choice

OBJECTIVES

- Students will practice listening skills
- Students will be able to understand how individual perceptions vary
- Students will learn about the differences of cultures through food, spices
- Students will organize and carry out a group project

ESSENTIAL QUESTIONS

- What can spices say about oneself?
- How is one perceived in the world?

CORE STANDARDS

II. Time, Continuity, and Change

III. People, Places, and Environments

IV. Individual Development and Identity

X. Civic Ideals and Practices

GRADE LEVEL

6TH-12TH

TIME FRAME

1-2 CLASS PERIODS

SUGGESTIONS:

- PRESENTATION PREPARATION: 20 MIN.
- PRESENTATION: 5-7 MIN. PER GROUP

MATERIALS

- GCV VIDEOS
  - RUHEL ISLAM
  - SHEGITU KEBEDE
  - BARBARA PIERRE-LOUIS
  - TEACHER'S CHOICE
- 2 IMMIGRANT STORY WORKSHEETS
- NOTEBOOK
- PEN, PENCILS
- SPICES FROM THE SPICE SIGNS CHART
- TIMER
- T-CHART

VIDEO LINKS

BARBARA G. PIERRE-LOUIS
www.greencardvoices.com/speakers/barbara-pierre-louis

RUHEL ISLAM
www.greencardvoices.com/speakers/ruhel-islam

SHEGITU KEBEDE
www.greencardvoices.com/speakers/shegitu-kebede

INSTRUCTIONS

PRIOR KNOWLEDGE: Follow these instructions before beginning the lesson.

- Bring the different spices (as shown in handout)
- Make copies of spice signs (handout)
- Cut spices signs (as many as you need for spice groups)
- Put the spice sign in a bowl

For the Teacher's Choice video, choose any spice from the country of that person

BE AWARE OF THE POSSIBILITY OF FOOD ALLERGIES.

BEFORE

1. Have students smell the spices from the handout. Have them write down the first thing that comes to mind.

2. Ask students the following questions:

- Do you have a favorite spice?
- If so, how often do you eat it? Which food do you eat it with?
- Where are Mr. Islam, Ms. Kebede, and Ms. Pierre-Louis from?
- What spice(s) do you think they would like?

3. Form 3-4 groups with a equal balance of students who watched videos for Mr. Islam, Ms. Kebede, and Ms. Pierre-Louis. In 3 minutes, students share their worksheet with their group and create one collective worksheet that captures all ideas. Each student must have a copy of the collective worksheet. Each group will present their collective worksheet in 2 minutes or less.

INSTRUCTIONS

DURING

4. Watch the GCV videos for Ruhel Islam, Shegitu Kebede, Barbara G. Pierre-Louis, and the teacher's choice. Go through the **VIDEO CONTENT DISCUSSION** questions as a class.

5. Pass the bowl of spice signs around and ask students to pick one sign (see **PRIOR KNOWLEDGE** section on the previous page). Direct learners to meet up with the other students with the same spice. Give each group their corresponding spice. Group members will smell their spice and discuss their experiences and thoughts.

6. Each spice group will deliver a 2-3 minutes presentation on their spice. Students can use whatever is available in the class to spice up their presentation. Instruct students to use the T-chart as a point of reference for their presentations.

AFTER

7. At the end of the activity:
- Have groups present to the class
- Have students discuss their group skills and reflect on their learning

MR. ISLAM

Where is Mr. Islam from?
How did Mr. Islam sustain his life in Bangladesh?
When did Mr. Islam arrive in the United States?
What happened to Mr. Islam in 2008?
What happened to Mr. Islam on March 13th, 2012?
How does he contribute to the United States?

MS. KEBEDE

Where is Ms. Kebede from?
What happened to Ms. Kebede at the age of 5? Where did she go?
How many brothers does Ms. Kebede have?
What happened to Ms. Kebede's older brother?
What strategy did Ms. Kebede use to protect her youngest brothers?
What happened to her brothers?
Describe Ms. Kebede's journey to the refugee camp.
Describe the circumstances of her departure from Kenya.
What was Ms. Kebede's life in North Dakota?
What gives Ms. Kebede hope?
How does Ms. Kebede contribute to the United States?

MS. PIERRE-LOUIS

How did immigration happen for Mrs. Pierre-Louis' family?
Who did Mrs. Pierre-Louis live with after her parents left?
What was Mrs. Pierre-Louis referring to when she said "I wasn't ready to learn"?
What were the living conditions when Mrs. Pierre-Louis reunited with her parents?
How many languages does Mrs. Pierre-Louis speak?
What is Mrs. Pierre-Louis message to students?
How does Mrs. Pierre-Louis contribute to the United States?

SUGGESTED FIELD TRIP

Prepare field trip – it can be done as a separate class activity. Contact Green Card Voices for help with planning and/or funding this field trip.

It might be stimulating for students' learning to plan a field trip to one of the restaurants. It will be an opportunity for students to try different foods and experience another culture.

To prepare for the field trip, put students in 3-4 groups. Each group must pick one out of the 8 questions listed below and say why they decided on that question and what do they want to learn. It is the ONLY question they ask to the restaurant owner; take good notes because they will have to report back to the larger group. No question can be duplicated!

GROUP FORMATIONS

First group to agree on a question from the list below gets that question.

OR

Students prepare an argument for the reason they want to pick a particular question. The entire class awards the question to the group with the best argument.

1. Tell us about your life in the country of your birth.
2. Tell us when you decided that you would be moving to the U.S.
3. Tell us the reasons you left your country of origin and why did you choose to come to the U.S.
4. How did you come to the U.S. (sketch out the route of your journey)?
5. What did you have to go through or even give up by leaving your country of origin?
6. Describe what it was like when you first arrived; what kind of obstacles or challenges did you face in the U.S.?
7. Describe your life in the U.S. currently.
8. What would you consider to be your personal contribution to your new community in the U.S.?

Profile:
RUHEL ISLAM

FROM: Sylhet, Bangladesh   CURRENT CITY: Minneapolis, MN
OCCUPATION: Restaurant Owner

Upon the request of his sister, who was moving to the U.S. with an American-businessman, and due to the hostile political climate of his home country, Mr. Islam left Bangladesh for the U.S. in 1996.

The fourth of seven children, he moved from his rural, childhood village of Sylhet to a larger urban area in pursuit of a college degree in commerce and accounting. Upon the completion of his degree and while still in Bangladesh, he started a farm – growing it from just two chickens to over two thousand.

Bringing his resourcefulness and self-reliance to the U.S., Mr. Islam opened his own restaurant: The Ghandi Mahal. His restaurant's menu is comprised solely of ingredients grown in his community gardens or purchased locally, demonstrating his commitment to environmentalism and sustainability.

Mr. Islam is also active in the local community. He was recently invited to visit the White House, meeting with the President and other senior staff members to both recognize his outstanding contributions as well as to engage in roundtable discussions regarding small business job creation. He lives in Minneapolis, MN and is happily married with three daughters.

For additional information, visit: www.gandhimahal.com

Sylhet, Bangladesh

Profile:
SHEGITU KEBEDE

FROM: Awasa, Ethiopia   CURRENT CITY: St. Paul, MN

OCCUPATION: Restaurant Owner

Despite the many trials and hardships during her life, Ms. Kebede's spirit remains strong.

Born in Awasa, Ethiopia, Ms. Kebede was surrounded by war during her early life. Orphaned at the age of five, she moved into an orphanage with her three brothers. However, the missionaries were forced to flee the country when violence from the civil war escalated. Like many young men in the region, Ms. Kebede's oldest brother was abducted to fight. Not wanting her two younger brothers to suffer the same fate, she married at the age of sixteen to provide them some protection.

Ms. Kebede was separated from family for a third time when she began a grueling, three-month journey to Kenya while pregnant. After a brief time in a Kenyan prison, Ms. Kebede gave birth to her son in a refugee camp. Two years later, she was eligible for a refugee resettlement in the United States. While her application was initially rejected, Ms. Kebede appealed the decision and was granted refugee status.

Ms. Kebede found tremendous success as an entrepreneur. She founded Going Home, Inc.—a program that provides job training for immigrant women—and Homework Center, which offered homework assistance and afterschool activities for immigrant children. Ms. Kebede was given the Virginia McKnight Binger Award in Human Services. She co-owns Flamingo Restaurant, serving authentic, East African cuisine. She is a published author and a motivational speaker, sharing her story with others.

For additional information, visit: www.flamingorestaurantmn.com

Profile:
BARBARA G. PIERRE-LOUIS

FROM: Pétionville, Haiti   CURRENT CITY: Oakdale, MN
OCCUPATION: Educator

Barbara G. Pierre-Louis loved the local color in Haiti: the variety of tropical flavors, the rhythmic music, and more. She missed these things when she left but learned to love her new home. She uses these experiences and her role as an educator to open the minds of her students.

Born in Pétionville—a suburb of Port-au-Prince—Ms. Pierre-Louis was raised by her extended family after her parents went to the U.S. to find better opportunities. While she enjoyed living among her relatives and the lively Haitian culture, life in her home country had its share of struggles. Living in a home with extended family sometimes meant that there was not always enough food to go around.

At the age of seven, an aunt applied for a visa on behalf of Ms. Pierre-Louis. It was approved, and she flew to Miami, Florida to reunite with her parents. It took some time for Barbara to adjust to life in the U.S. Her family lived in a cramped, one-bedroom apartment, and everything about America seemed strange—smells, food, language. School was particularly difficult. Ms. Pierre-Louis struggled with a language barrier and was bullied by her peers for being "different."

After high school, Ms. Pierre-Louis attended the University of Florida for her undergraduate studies. Following that she earned her Master's and PhD degrees from the University of Minnesota where she studied Spanish and Portuguese studies. Currently, Ms. Pierre-Louis is an educator at Metropolitan State University in the Twin Cities. Barbara lives in St. Paul with her husband and two children.

Pétionville, Haiti

WHAT'S YOUR SPICE

Spice Signs

Shegitu's Spice

Garlic & Ginger

Teacher's Choice Spice

Barbara's Spice

Star Anise

Ruhel's Spice

Turmeric

Encouraging Participation

LOOKS LIKE	SOUNDS LIKE
Smiles	What's your idea?
Eye contact	Awesome!
Thumbs up	Good idea.
Pack on back	That's interesting.

Checking For Understanding

LOOKS LIKE	SOUNDS LIKE
Eye contact	Explain that to me please.
Leaning Forward	Can you show me?
Interested Expression	How did you get that answer?
Open Gestures and Posture	Give me an example.
	How would you explain it to a teacher?

Summarizing

LOOKS LIKE	SOUNDS LIKE
Leaning Forwards	Let's review what we've said...
Pleasant Expression	Our key ideas seem to be...
Open Gestures and Posture	At this point, we have...
	The points we've made so far are...

Chart reproduced from "The nuts and bolts of cooperative learning" 1994
David W. Johnson, Roger T. Johnson, Edythe Johnson Holubec

LESSON 5: I AM FROM ...

FOCUS

- Use a genealogy report to reconstruct the past
- Use of clues and research
- Thinking creatively, outside the box

GRADE LEVEL

6TH-12TH

TIME FRAME

1-2 CLASS PERIODS

MATERIALS

- REPORT FROM LESSON 2
- NOTEBOOK
- PENS, PENCILS

OBJECTIVES

- Students will apply critical thinking skills to reconstruct a story
- Students will use appropriate strategies to organize their research
- Students will create a fiction story

ESSENTIAL QUESTIONS

- What's your story?
- What's your identity?

CORE STANDARDS

I. Culture and Cultural Diversity

II. Time, Continuity, and Change

III. People, Places, and Environments

IV. Individual Development and Identity

VI. Poverty, Authority, and Governance

IX. Global Connections

INSTRUCTIONS

BEFORE

1. Review **LESSON 2: I AM HERE AND I MATTER** with the class.

2. Instruct students to use the information they've gathered from their reports for the following activity.

DURING

3. Tell students to imagine a possible story, for at least two of their ancestors, based on the GCV videos they've watched thus far. Students can use the list of ancestry websites on the following page as a resource for this assignment. It is not an exhaustive list so feel free to make additions to it.

4. Have students research why their ancestors might have left their countries (the push factors) and why their ancestors came to the United States (the pull factors). If students don't know what the pull and push factors are, they can research the topic and read people's stories (from their ancestors' country) who came to United States around the same time. If students know a movie about the subject, they can also watch it. The idea is to create a story their ancestors would be proud of.

AFTER

5. For next class, give assignment below:

Students should revise and edit their stories at home, and come prepared to share with the class the following class period.

HOMEWORK

- Watch the GCV story for Miguel Ramos

- Fill out the Immigration Story Worksheet for Miguel Ramos

ANCESTRY WEBPAGES

NATIVE AMERICAN ANCESTRY

www.indians.org/articles/native-american-indians.html

AFRICAN AMERICAN ANCESTRY

www.pbs.org/wnet/slavery/timeline/index.html

CHINESE AMERICAN ANCESTRY

http://1.usa.gov/1IKABl4

HMONG AMERICAN ANCESTRY

www.epodunk.com/ancestry/Hmong.html

www.angelfire.com/in/Laos/AsianHistory.html

JAPANESE AMERICAN ANCESTRY

http://1.usa.gov/XS2LX8

VIETNAMESE AMERICAN ANCESTRY

www.migrationpolicy.org/article/vietnamese-immigrants-united-states

EUROPEAN AMERICAN ANCESTRY

http://teacher.scholastic.com/activities/immigration/tour/

The Statue of Liberty and Ellis Island

ASSESSMENT: WHAT WE LEARNED FROM THE STORIES

First, play a GCV video you have not yet watched with the class. Play the video 2-3 times. Students can only start writing after the second viewing.

1. What are the positive/important facts I learned from the story?

2. In groups of 2-4, create a list of the top 5 positive facts. What are they?

3. What is the important information we learn about immigration from the story?

4. What do these facts/information tell us about the person in the video? About immigration?

5. How is this video different from the other stories we've watched?

FOCUS

- Identify and describe challenges immigrants face
- Recognize the struggles immigrants have
- Name the roles immigrants play in the economy

OBJECTIVES

- Students will use critical inquiry to reconstruct and interpret a story
- Students will identify the pull and push factors of immigration
- Students will generate questions and formulate ideas about immigration

GRADE LEVEL

6TH-12TH

TIME FRAME

1-2 CLASS PERIODS

MATERIALS

- MIGUEL RAMOS GCV VIDEO
- NOTEBOOK/PADS
- PENS, PENCILS, MARKERS
- ART SUPPLIES

ESSENTIAL QUESTIONS

- How do people in the United States label others?
- What are possible obstacles involved with the pursuit of the American dream?

CORE STANDARDS

I. Culture and Cultural Diversity

III. People, Places, and Environments

IV. Individual Development and Identity

VI. Poverty, Authority, and Governance

IX. Global Connections

VIDEO LINKS

MIGUEL RAMOS

www.greencardvoices.com/speakers/miguel-ramos/

INSTRUCTIONS

PRIOR KNOWLEDGE: Discuss the following questions with the classroom

- Where does Mr. Ramos work?
- Have you ever gone to a baseball game?

- Have you traveled abroad?
- How do people treat you when you travel to another country?
- How does that make you feel?

BEFORE

1. Watch the GCV video for Mr. Ramos.

2. Have students fill out the "Who Am I" worksheet. They may do so while watching the video or after it has finished.

INSTRUCTIONS

DURING

3. After watching the video, discuss the following questions:

- Where is Mr. Ramos from?
- What's the story behind the baseball glove?
- What happened when Mr. Ramos turned 17?
- What's Mr. Ramos commitment for life?
- What did Mr. Ramos like about Minnesota?
- What struggles did Mr. Ramos face 20 years ago?
- What does it means being an "alien"?
- How does Mr. Ramos contribute to the United States?
- How did Mr. Ramos feel about being labeled?
- Would you be able to retell Mr. Ramos' story?
- What made immigrating difficult for Mr. Ramos? What could have helped?

4. Using a large sheet or paper or a blackboard, create a T-chartof the answers generated from the final question "What made it difficult? What could have helped?"

5. Have students discuss how their answers compare and contrast the answers given during the **PRIOR KNOWLEDGE** discussion.

6. Ask students what else they would like to know and what questions they would ask Mr. Ramos if they met him.

AFTER

7. For next class:

- Ask students to write down their questions and submit them the next class period.
- Ask student research their favorite thing they learned from Mr. Ramos' story.

Worksheet:

WHO AM I?

Originally from _____ (city, state), _____ (name) came to Minnesota thinking he was ready for the drastic change. He realized that many challenges were before him, but he has never given up on his dream.

_____ (name) grew up in a _____ (adjective) household in _____ (city, state). When he was seventeen years old, his father passed away; his family _____ (auxiliary verb, verb) a funeral. _____ (name) promised himself that his future family would have the best opportunities possible. As he grew older, _____ (name) began his career in _____ (city, state). One summer, _____ (name) visited _____ (city, state). He was amazed by the opportunities he saw and knew it was the place where he could fulfill his promise.

Despite his success in _____ (city, state), _____ (name) had to restart his career from _____ (noun). Never giving up, he applied to become the _____ (name of an organization) of a local nonprofit. He was later appointed by the governor to serve on the Juvenile Justice Advisory Committee. In 2000, _____ (name) was selected as one of Minneapolis/ St. Paul Magazines' "100 People to Watch." He also received the 2011 Diversity in Business Award from the Minneapolis/St. Paul Business Journal. In 2009, he was offered a position with the Minnesota Twins as their _____ (name of a position) Director and has been working there ever since. In addition to chairing the board of Green Card Voices, he has served on the board of directors for the Greater Minneapolis & St. Paul United Way, Science Museum of Minnesota and Casa de Esperanza.

AN HOUR WITH: _____

Contact Green Card Voices to request a speaker at least a month in advance. To make sure that students are prepared for the visit, ask them to write a list of questions they could have for an immigrant they might meet. Using these questions for students, create discussion notes for the upcoming visit. Provide the immigrant with students' questions, so that s/he can prepare and answer them during the visit.

Confirm date with GCV and tell students when the immigrant will come. Before the immigrant visit, share the discussion notes and inform the immigrant what topics you would like to also address. During the visit, moderate a discussion between students and the immigrant based on the discussion notes.

LESSON 7: VISIT FROM A STORYTELLER

FOCUS

- Interact with an immigrant
- Recognizing cultural differences

OBJECTIVES

- Students will interact with an immigrant
- Students will apply the T-Chart strategies
- Students will identify the pull and push factors of immigration

ESSENTIAL QUESTIONS

- What are the reasons a person might have for leaving their home country?

CORE STANDARDS

I. Culture and Cultural Diversity

III. People, Places, and Environments

IV. Individual Development and Identity

VIII. Science, Technology, and Society

INSTRUCTIONS

LESSON 7

BEFORE

1. Contact Green Card Voices if you need help finding a guest storyteller for this lesson. Meet with your storyteller to determine how long his/her presentation will be. Inform your guest that there will be a Question & Answer section after their presentation.

2. Discuss the following questions with the class:

What language(s) does our guest speak besides English?

Do you (the students) speak a language other than English?

How do you feel when you speak a language other than your native language?

How do you feel when you hear others speak in a language other than your own?

DURING

2. Tell students to listen attentively to the storyteller's presentation.

3. Instruct students to write down 2-3 questions they have for the storyteller while s/he is giving his/her presentation.

4. After the presentation, inform students that there will be Q&A session and to ask one of the questions they have for the storyteller.

AFTER

5. Have your students write a brief thank you note for your storyteller.

Tony Oliva, Cuba

LESSON 8: PERSEVERANCE – PART 1

FOCUS

- Creating a welcoming environment
- Empathizing with others

OBJECTIVES

- Students will identify welcoming attitudes
- Students will imagine how they would interact with a new immigrant student
- Students will name at least one country from previous lessons

ESSENTIAL QUESTIONS

- Is our school welcoming?
- What collective actions can we take to make our school more welcoming?

CORE STANDARDS

I. Culture and Cultural Diversity

III. People, Places, and Environments

IV. Individual Development and Identity

GRADE LEVEL

6TH-12TH

TIME FRAME

1-2 CLASS PERIODS

MATERIALS

- IBRAHIM HIRSI GCV VIDEO
- IMMIGRANT STORY WORKSHEET
- K-W-L LEARNING TOOL NOTEBOOK/PADS
- PENS, PENCILS, MARKERS

VIDEO LINKS

IBRAHIM HIRSI

www.greencardvoices.com/speakers/ibrahim-hirsi

INSTRUCTIONS

LESSON 8

IF ANY OF YOUR STUDENTS HAVE BEEN HELD BACK A GRADE, MEET WITH THEM BEFORE CLASS TO MAKE SURE THEY ARE COMFORTABLE DURING THIS LESSON.

PRIOR KNOWLEDGE: Suggested questions for students

- What age are you in 9th grade?
- How would you feel if you were held back a year in school?
- How would you want your classmates to behave towards you?

BEFORE

1. Instruct students fill out the **K-W-L** worksheet. Have them think about what they've learned during the previous lessons.

DURING

2. Watch Mr. Hirsi's GCV video. Instruct students to fill out the immigrant story worksheet for Mr. Hirsi.

3. Re-watch Mr. Hirsi's GCV video. Tell students to take notes focusing on the following:

- How did the video make you feel?
- How did the video make you think?

4. Inform students to take good notes during a video. They will eventually write a 2-page letter or create a comic book. The purpose of the assignment is for students to think about what they would do if a student like Mr. Hirsi joined their class.

INSTRUCTIONS

AFTER

5. For next class, ask students to submit a proposal about the theme or topic of their 2-page letter or comic book. Have your students think about a hypothetical student that joined their class. Student can make a proposal individually or in groups.

Instructions for the proposal:

- Country the student is from and why they choose that particular country
- Language the student speaks besides English
- Pull and push factors that affected the student
- The age of the student
- Student grade level
- Does the student have working knowledge of English
- How they envision helping the student

Examples of topics they can choose to address:

- How to make the student feel welcome
- Things they can teach the student, e.g. how to open a locker, the layout of school
- Help with homework

Profile:
IBRAHIM HIRSI

FROM: Mogadishu, Somalia   **CURRENT CITY:** Minneapolis, MN

OCCUPATION: Journalist

Ibrahim Hirsi's story is one of incredible perseverance. Upon leaving his home country of Somalia, it took him nearly fifteen years to reach the United States.

Mr. Hirsi was born in Mogadishu, the seventh of ten children. At the time of his birth, in 1986, political tensions were brewing. Four years later, Ibrahim and his family moved to Kenya in response to civil war. His family began the process of immigrating to the United States shortly thereafter, and by August of 2001 they had completed the interviews and security screenings required; everything was in order. Then came the events of September 11, 2001 – Ibrahim's journey to the U.S. was to be delayed for another four years.

While others close to him set aside their ambitions to leave Kenya, Mr. Hirsi was not discouraged and continued preparing for a life in the United States. Incredibly, after finally reaching the U.S. in 2005 and entering high school as an 18-year-old freshman, he completed all of the credits required for graduation in just two years.

Ibrahim went on to graduate from the University of Minnesota with a journalism degree, and he is now both a communications assistant and writer at Wallin Education Partners as well as a regular contributor to the Twin Cities Daily Planet.

For more information, visit: www.minnpost.com

Mogadishu, Somalia

Name: _____

Date: _____

LESSON 8

K-W-L LEARNING TOOL

K	W	L
What I **K**now	What I **W**ant to know	What we **L**earned
Use your notebook to list what you already know about immigration	What else would you like to learn? List any questions you might have	Use your class assignment to list what you've learned

Adapted from: Ogle, D. M. (1986). KWL: A teaching model that develops active reading of expository text. The reading teacher, 564-570.

GCV

IMMIGRANT STORY WORKSHEET

I listened to the story of...	
S/he was born in city/country/continent...	
The reason(s) s/he left the country of origin	
Education completed in the country of origin and in the U.S.	
Who s/he left behind; who came with to the U.S.	
Current Occupation	

What was his/her biggest surprise when s/he came to the U.S.?

How did s/he cope with the new environment?

How does s/he contribute to the new homeland?

LESSON 8: PERSEVERANCE - PART 2

FOCUS

- Creating a welcoming environment
- Empathizing with others
- Recognizing the perception and challenges immigrants face

OBJECTIVES

- Students will identify welcoming attitudes
- Students will imagine how they would interact with a new immigrant student
- Students will name at least one country from previous lessons

ESSENTIAL QUESTIONS

- Is our school welcoming?
- What collective actions can we take to make our school more welcoming?

CORE STANDARDS

I. Culture and Cultural Diversity

III. People, Places, and Environments

IV. Individual Development and Identity

GRADE LEVEL

6TH-12TH

TIME FRAME

1 CLASS PERIOD

MATERIALS

- NOTE CARD
- NOTEBOOK/PADS
- PENS, PENCILS, MARKERS

NOTES

Compile students' K-W-L sheets and have them available for them class.

INSTRUCTIONS

PRIOR KNOWLEDGE: Suggested questions for students

- What did you learn in **LESSON 8: PART 1**?
- Was it easy or difficult to write your proposal?
- What made it easy or difficult?

- What country did you choose?
- Let's list some of the pull factors you used.
- Let's list some of the push factors you used.

BEFORE

1. Instruct students to write the name of a country from a previous lesson on a notecard. Students form groups based on the countries they have chosen.

2. In their group, instruct students to share their proposal from **LESSON 8: PART 1** for 10 minutes. Reminder: their proposal is for a 2-page letter or a comic book that describes how students would welcome a new immigrant student.

3. Students can decide if they would like to work individually or in a group to write their 2-page letter or create their comic book.

DURING

4. For 30 minutes, groups and/or individuals will create their letter or comic book based on their proposal. Tell students when 10 minutes remain so they can finish their projects.

AFTER

5. Assist students in taping their letters and/or comic books on a wall in the classroom or in the hallway, if possible.

6. For Lesson 9, reserve the computer lab.

LESSON 9: LEARNING WITH OTHERS

FOCUS

- Explore cultural values
- Deepen understanding of others
- Presentation skills

OBJECTIVES

- Students will name push and pull factors
- Students will apply the **K-W-L** note taking strategy
- Students will name at least one country from previous lessons

ESSENTIAL QUESTIONS

- What are the circumstances that may cause people to leave their country of origin?
- What does it mean to start your life over?

CORE STANDARDS

I. Culture and Cultural Diversity

III. People, Places, and Environments

IV. Individual Development and Identity

GRADE LEVEL
6TH-12TH

TIME FRAME
1-2 CLASS PERIODS

MATERIALS

- GCV VIDEO OF KUSHE SAW
- IMMIGRANT STORY WORKSHEET
- MS. SAW VIDEO CONTENT DISCUSSION WORKSHEET
- STICKY PADS/NOTEBOOK
- K-W-L LEARNING TOOL
- PENS, PENCILS, MARKERS
- COMPUTER LAB

VIDEO LINKS

KUSHE SAW
www.greencardvoices.com/speakers/kushe-saw

INSTRUCTIONS

LESSON 9

PRIOR KNOWLEDGE: Suggested questions for students

- What did **LESSON 8** teach you about the challenges immigrants face?
- Was it easy or difficult to write your proposal?
- What made it easy? What made it difficult?
- What country did you choose?
- Can you list some of the pull factors you used?
- Can you list some of the push factors you used?

BEFORE

1. Watch Ms. Saw's video.
   - Instruct students to fill out an immigrant story worksheet for Ms. Saw.
2. Watch Ms. Saw's video again.
   - Tell students to take good notes using the **K-W-L** tool.
   - Hand out Ms. Saw's Video Content Discussion worksheet
3. Watch Ms. Saw's video a third time
   - Instruct students to fill out Ms. Saw's Video Content Discussion worksheet
4. Move to the computer lab. Students will be researching topics for an in-class presentation.

INSTRUCTIONS

DURING

5. Have students prepare a presentation based on their worksheets. Students can choose to work in groups or individually.

- Students will use the **K-W-L LEARNING TOOL** to organize their questions (presentation will follow the **K-W-L LEARNING TOOL**).

- Students will research topics from their **W** sections of the **K-W-L LEARNING TOOL** to enrich their presentations.

AFTER

6. At the end of the class, instruct students to finish preparing their presentations at home and be ready to present the following class period.

7. For Lesson 10, reserve the computer lab.

NOTES

For the next class, plan ample time for students' presentations.

Tell students to think about actions they can take to improve immigrants' lives.

HOMEWORK

Encourage students to research about the Dream Act on this website:

dreamact.info

Profile:
KUSHE SAW

FROM: Rangoon, Burma   CURRENT CITY: St. Paul, MN
OCCUPATION: Nursing Assistant

Kushe Saw spent much of her childhood in the jungles of Burma, hiding from Burmese soldiers in the area. Even when she was at school, Kushe and her teachers would hide in the foliage. In comparison, the U.S. was a haven of safety and opportunity.

Born in 1971, Ms. Saw grew up during an era of civil war and military dictatorship. When she was only four years old, Kushe's parents left her under her grandfather's care. A pastor and avid gardener, Kushe's grandfather had a profound impact on her life. One Sunday, Burmese soldiers attempted to overtake her grandfather's church but failed. The soldiers returned that evening to torch the village. Since then, Kushe was constantly on the move.

After her parents died, Kushe was adopted by a Karen couple. Her adoptive father heard of a UN program in Thailand that was evacuating refugees from Burma; they decided to apply. The application process was no easy task. Kushe's adoptive family was applying for ten people without any kind of legal identification. Fortunately, their application to move to the U.S. was approved, and Ms. Saw came to Louisiana in 1999.

Since then, Ms. Saw received her nursing assistant certification from the International Institute of Minnesota, an organization that helps transitioning immigrants. She works at St. Anthony Park Home and hopes to one day become a registered nurse. Kushe lives in St. Paul with her husband and their three children.

Rangoon, Burma

Name: _____

Date: _____

1. Describe Ms. Saw's life in Burma

2. What significant events happened to Ms. Saw on a Sunday?

3. What circumstances led to her coming to the U.S.?

4. When did she arrive in the U.S.?

5. Did she come directly to Minnesota? Why did she choose Minnesota?

6. What struggles did she face when she moved to the U.S.?

7. Did she need to learn anything?

8. Does she have any children? If so, how many?

9. Are her children active in any activities?

10. What's her current occupation?

11. Why did she choose that occupation?

12. What did you learn about Ms. Saw's life that is significantly different from your life?

13. How might you use this knowledge to improve immigrants' arrival in the U.S.?

14. In her story, was there anything that was similar to your life? If so, what was it?

15. How might this knowledge change your interaction with other immigrants?

LESSON 10: THE DREAM ACT

FOCUS

- Power structures
- Interdependence in immigration
- Watch Irma Márquez Trapero's GCV video

OBJECTIVES

- Students will research the Dream Act and the Executive Actions on Immigration
- Students will compare and contrast the Dream Act and the Executive Actions on Immigration
- Students will think about reforms to the new Executive Actions on immigration
- Students will write a letter to their successors

ESSENTIAL QUESTIONS

- What does it mean being a citizen?
- How can the immigration system improve?

CORE STANDARDS

VI. Power, Authority, and Governance

IX. Global Connections

X. Civic Ideals and Practices

GRADE LEVEL

8TH-12TH

TIME FRAME

1-3 CLASS PERIODS

MATERIALS

- GCV VIDEO OF IRMA MÁRQUEZ TRAPERO
- IMMIGRANT STORY WORKSHEET
- STICKY PADS/NOTEBOOK
- K-W-L LEARNING TOOL
- PENS, PENCILS, MARKERS
- COMPUTER LAB

VIDEO LINKS

IRMA MARQUEZ TRAPERO
www.greencardvoices.com/speakers/irma-marquez-trapero

INSTRUCTIONS

LESSON 10

YOU MAY HAVE UNDOCUMENTED STUDENTS IN YOUR CLASSROOM. BE SENSITIVE TO THIS DURING CLASS DISCUSSIONS. THEY MAY BE HESITANT OR RELUCTANT TO PARTICIPATE.

> **PRIOR KNOWLEDGE:** Suggested questions for students. Use a world map to help facilitate the discussion.
> - Who has ever been to Mexico?
> - Where is Mexico?
> - Do you know anyone who is from Mexico?
> - As an American, what do you need to travel to Mexico?

BEFORE

1. Students will do their presentations from **LESSON 9**.

2. Watch Ms. Irma Márquez Trapero's video. Instruct students to fill out the immigrant story worksheet.

3. After the video, discuss the following questions:
   - What degree does Irma's mother have?
   - What was the catalyst for Irma's immigration to the United States?
   - When did Irma arrive in the United States?
   - How long did it take for Irma and her family to receive their documents?
   - Did Irma's family intend to move back to Mexico?
   - Why couldn't they return home?
   - What job do Irma's parents have in the United States?
   - What is deferred action?
   - When did Irma receive her work authorization card?
   - How does Irma feel about being able to contribute to the United States?

INSTRUCTIONS

DURING

4. Move to the computer lab

5. Instruct students to research about the Dream Act at DREAMACT.INFO and the executive actions on immigration at WWW.USCIS.GOV/IMMIGRATIONACTION

6 Have students answer the following:

- Compare and contrast Illegal vs. Undocumented immigrants
- Name at least 3 changes from the Dream Act to the Deferred Action for Parental Accountability (DAPA)
- Is the new reform (Executive Actions on immigration) better than the old reform? If yes, state why.
- How would the new reform help Ms. Márquez Trapero?
- What else could you add to improve the new reform?
- What is the estimated number of undocumented immigrants in the United States?
- Are immigration reforms fair? Why or why not?

AFTER

7. Instruct students to further research and answer the following questions:

- How did immigration happen before Ellis Island?
- What happen in 1492?
- How did the United States become a nation of immigrants?
- Why should there be laws or reforms now? Do you think the laws/reforms are fair?

LESSON 10

Profile:
IRMA MÁRQUEZ TRAPERO

FROM: Culiacan, Mexico   CURRENT CITY: Minneapolis, MN
OCCUPATION: Legal Assistant

In fourth grade, Irma Márquez-Trapero packed for a two-year stay in the United States; it was their last resort. When those two years passed, her family did not want to leave; they stayed in the country with lapsed passports and without work eligibility. Suddenly, being undocumented formed their identity.

During her early childhood, Irma lived in a nice community and was raised by two parents who were happily employed. After her brother was born, however, her mother could not find an employer willing to accept a woman with significant family obligations. In an effort to find better opportunities, they planned to move in with Irma's uncle in the United States.

Despite her many obstacles, Ms. Márquez-Trapero has been incredibly grateful for the opportunities she has had since living in the United States. With her parents working factory jobs at a meatpacking facility and facing the threat of deportation, Irma was inspired to do her best at school and help her family navigate their new world's language and institutions.

Just before graduating college, Irma received a social security number from the Deferred Action for Childhood Arrivals program, granting her employment eligibility. However, Deferred Action provides only temporary relief—a two-year program with the option to reapply. Her future in the United States is uncertain, but she is on a path set for citizenship. Ms. Márquez-Trapero has already begun working in the field of immigration law. Through her career, she hopes to carry out her passion of being a role model and advisor to fellow immigrants.

Culiacan, Mexico

Name: _____

Date: _____

IMMIGRANT STORY WORKSHEET

I listened to the story of...	
S/he was born in city/country/continent...	
The reason(s) s/he left the country of origin	
Education completed in the country of origin and in the U.S.	
Who s/he left behind; who came with to the U.S.	
Current Occupation	

What was his/her biggest surprise when s/he came to the U.S.?

How did s/he cope with the new environment?

How does s/he contribute to the new homeland?

LETTERS TO THE SUCCESSORS

Students will write a letter that will be given to new students who will take this class after them. The letter should tell future students what they should know in order to enjoy this class.

INSTRUCT STUDENTS TO:

1. Write a clean copy of their letter.
2. If they want, they can sign their name.
3. Hand the completed letter back to you for distribution to future students.

SOME TOPICS STUDENTS CAN WRITE ABOUT ARE:

1. What I know about this course that I wish I'd known when I started
2. The most important thing I did to succeed in the class
3. What I enjoyed most about this class
4. Something new I learned in the class
5. Something important I learned and really want to share.

IF STUDENTS NEED HELP WRITING THEIR LETTERS, HAVE THEM FOLLOW THIS TEMPLATE.

Dear Future Student,

One thing I wish I'd known when we started this unit is...

One thing I think you should know about immigration is...

The most important thing I did to succeed in this unit was...

My favorite part of this unit was...

Something new I learned was...

Something important I learned and really want to share is...

GRADE LEVEL
6TH-12TH

TIME FRAME
1-2 CLASS PERIODS

MATERIALS

- STICKY PADS/NOTEBOOK
- PENS, PENCILS, MARKERS

HOMEWORK

Students can write a brief paper about what they wished they had known prior to doing this unit on immigration and if/how their views on immigration have changed.

Adapted from "Letter to the successors" Brookfield, S. D., & Brookfield, S. (1995). *Becoming a Critically Reflective Teacher.*

LINKS TO VIDEOS

MARY GORŠE MANNING
www.greencardvoices.com/speakers/mary-gorse-manning/

NACHITO HERRERA
www.greencardvoices.com/speakers/nachito-herrera/

NICKOLAI KOLAROV
www.greencardvoices.com/speakers/nickolai-kolarov/

IKHLAQ HUSSAIN
www.greencardvoices.com/speakers/ikhlaq-hussain

BARBARA G. PIERRE-LOUIS
www.greencardvoices.com/speakers/barbara-pierre-louis/

RUHEL ISLAM
www.greencardvoices.com/speakers/ruhel-islam/

SHEGITU KEBEDE
www.greencardvoices.com/speakers/shegitu-kebede/

MIGUEL RAMOS
www.greencardvoices.com/speakers/miguel-ramos/

KUSHE SAW
www.greencardvoices.com/speakers/kushe-saw/

IBRAHIM HIRSI
www.greencardvoices.com/speakers/ibrahim-hirsi/

IRMA MARQUEZ TRAPERO
www.greencardvoices.com/speakers/irma-marquez-trapero/

41985139R00044

Made in the USA
Middletown, DE
28 March 2017